First Job, New Career, Now What?

23 Tips for Guaranteed Career Success

MORINEE TERRY

DEDICATION

To my niece Kiera who has excelled in college. May you be even more successful in your professional career pursuits.
Instagram: @kieraplease
YouTube: @kieraplease

To my husband Richard who has always encouraged me and who has never complained about all of the times he has had to fix Kiera's computer. And no, I don't know why her laptop looks like the dog chewed on it.

CONTENTS

INTRODUCTION

Ever realize you don't know what you don't know, but if you did know, you could and would do something about it? Sounds a bit complicated but it's not. Often, the most meaningful career advice is simple, sincere, and within your immediate control to do something about.

FIRST JOB, NEW CAREER, NOW WHAT? 23 Tips for Guaranteed Career Success shares advice managers rarely take the time to give but which has a huge impact on whether you excel in your career. It's the stuff you don't know that you don't know, but that you should know.

FIRST JOB, NEW CAREER, NOW WHAT? 23 Tips for Guaranteed Career Success provides twenty-three pieces of need-to-know career advice. The advice is within your control to act upon immediately and is sure to have a positive, long-term impact on your career. The advice is specifically aimed at young professionals just beginning their career or in their second role since college. It is also relevant for non-native Americans beginning their professional career with an American company.

#1 TAKE THE INITIATIVE.

Don't wait for your manager to tell you what work needs to be done. You *figure it out*, and just do it.

It's called initiative—determining what needs to be done and doing it without anyone telling you to do it.

Too often, we sit around waiting for instruction from someone telling us what work to do next, or we wait for permission or an invitation to get involved with work that we're interested in doing. The instructions are your job description and you received permission when you were hired.

Look around you. Take the initiative, figure out what needs to be done, and do it.

#2 ASK FOR FEEDBACK.

Learn to ask for feedback in a way that affirms the good work you're doing, while at the same time creating an opportunity for honesty about areas where you need to improve.

It's challenging for people to give feedback, especially unsolicited feedback. To get meaningful information about your work performance, you must take responsibility for creating a safe environment where people can be honest with you.

Proactively ask for feedback—and listen to it. Let the person know up front that you will not argue with them, be offended by anything they share, or try to justify your actions. You may ask clarifying questions to gain insight and understanding. Your goals, however, are to hear and respect what they have to say, and to get input on how to improve your work performance.

#3 TAKE RESPONSIBILITY FOR YOUR PROFESSIONAL DEVELOPMENT.

Take responsibility for your professional development and career growth. If you don't, no one else will.

Contrary to popular belief and wishful thinking, your manager is not responsible for your professional development—*you are*. It is up to you to identify training opportunities, find training courses, and proactively ask your manager to allow you to work on assignments you're interested in doing.

It's nice to believe that your manager was placed into his or her position because they know how to nurture talent, but that's a myth. They got their job because they know how to get the work done. In general, it is your manager's responsibility to have the ubiquitous annual performance review conversation with you. However, once they file the paperwork associated with that check-the-box activity in human resources, managers rarely think about it again until MAYBE the next year—MAYBE. Your manager is busy thinking about what he or she needs to do to promote their career growth. Your career growth? Eh, not so much. That's up to you.

#4 ASK FOR AN ORG CHART.

Too often, we assume that because someone has manager or supervisor in their title, they have organizational power; that's not necessarily true.

An organizational chart will help you understand you/your manager's position in the organization *relative to* the other positions within the company. The org chart will provide a visual outline representing the degree of positional power someone has based on the location of his or her role on the org chart. In general, the closer someone's role is positioned relative to the primary leader of an organization, i.e., President, Vice Presidents, the greater their positional power. The more positional power someone has the greater their authority, influence, and ability to make decisions on behalf of the company.

In addition to understanding someone's positional

power, an organizational chart will help you become familiar with people's names and titles. At a minimum, it will make you aware of individuals with whom you may want to make a good impression or be careful not to offend.

#5 NEVER, EVER MAKE THE ADMIN ASSISTANT ANGRY.

Administrative assistants have positional power. Never, under any circumstance, get on their bad side. If you do, it will cost you dearly.

Also known as executive assistants and secretaries, the individuals in this role generally report into people who have positional power. Therefore, by association, admin assistants tend to have positional power too. In fact, an individual will have an admin assistant reporting directly to them only if they have some positional power within the company.

Admin assistants are often dismissed because people view their jobs as clerical and not critical to the core business operations. This is a big mistake. Admin assistants, by the nature of to whom they report, have access to important information, people in other

9

positions of power, and a hidden store of office supplies. In other words, they wield a significant amount of authority, influence and control.

Always be nice to the admin assistant, no matter what. Regardless of whether they have a sour disposition, seem angry all the time, or are one of the friendliest, most helpful people you know, be nice. They have the ear of people in powerful positions and control over office resources that you will need one day. Never underestimate their positional power.

#6 CREATE A DIVERSE SOCIAL NETWORK IN THE WORKPLACE.

At work, develop a diverse network of peers from other parts of the organization. Get to know colleagues who are roughly around your age and in positions relatively close to your level within the organization.

Peer networks can be great sources of useful information. Often one part of an organization will have access to information that has yet to reach the larger company population. Your 'workplace friends' from other functional areas can clue you in on this information (e.g., company gossip) prior to its announcement within the company. Knowing workplace information before everyone else can often prove to be invaluable.

At a minimum, create a peer network possessing the

basic traits of diversity—race, gender, and ethnicity. Different groups have access to information in varying degrees. The more diverse your peer network, the greater and richer the information to which you gain access. As you and your 'workplace friends' progress in your careers, hopefully you'll be able to nurture and maintain a relationship of trust with one another. And trust always trumps positional power.

#7 INTRODUCE YOURSELF.

Take the initiative and be the first one to extend a handshake and introduce yourself when you meet someone new.

Oftentimes we wait for someone to initiate introductions, after which we say hello but fail to shake hands and/or state our name along with our job title. You're a professional now, and part of getting people to see and treat you like a professional is acting like one. In every professional situation, *even if the situation appears casual,* when you encounter someone new, *introduce yourself like a professional.* Have the confidence to introduce yourself first by offering a firm handshake and stating your name, title and/or department. If they fail to respond with their name and/or title, ask them, and follow up with "Pleased to meet you."

#8 LEARN HOW TO BE PROFESSIONALLY ENGAGING AND LIKEABLE.

People like working with people they like. When coworkers like you, they are more willing to involve you in their work and to trust you with organizational information (e.g., company gossip).

You may have heard, "You don't have to like me, you just have to respect me." Respect goes a long way; however, being respected for the work that you do, <u>and</u> *being a pleasure to work* with will take you further. To be engaging in the work place, you must be willing to share some of your personal life with coworkers, because people trust people whom they feel they know. While some people 'don't want their personal business known at work', which is wise, it's important to have areas of your personal life that are open for sharing. Don't talk about your family drama; do talk about a funny childhood story. In general, what you share should be generic in nature, but come across as personal because it's about you. Additionally, be sure to smile often and laugh once in a while.

#9 DON'T DRINK WITH WORK COLLEAGUES.

When you are with work colleagues, you are always being assessed—*always*. It's easier to remember this when you're in an office setting, but you must also be mindful of this when you are at a work sponsored social event.

It's important that you remain alert and maintain your professional persona. You don't ever want to be so loose that your professional guard slips, your wits become dull, or anyone accuses you of not being able to hold your liquor. Have fun, relax, but always keep your professional guard up, your wits sharp, and restrict your drinking to when you are among real friends.

#10 DROP THE "YES MA'AM" AND "NO SIR".

Out of deference, you may have been brought up to address people older than you by using ma'am and sir. In a professional work environment, most people are called by their first name, regardless of their age or title. It does not matter whether they are older or have more work experience, they are your colleagues and you can address them using their first name unless otherwise instructed.

Additionally, people in servant positions often use ma'am and sir to address those they are serving. You are not a servant and, theoretically speaking, you are on equal grounds with all your colleagues. Drop the ma'am and sir from your work vocabulary.

#11 REFRAIN FROM DISCUSSING RACE, RELIGION, AND POLITICS.

Just because everyone else is discussing a subject does not mean you need to talk about it too.

Politics, race relations, and religion can be volatile subjects. Conversations involving these topics rarely leave all parties feeling warm and fuzzy toward one another at the end of the discussion. People defend their views passionately and often say things that would be better left unsaid in the work environment. Ignorant people don't want to be educated; they want to be right—*at your expense*. You don't want someone who doesn't agree with your views to hold it against you when assigning work, assessing your performance, or discussing you with someone else.

You might not agree with what is being said but keep your cool, tell them "No comment," disengage from the conversation, and walk on.

#12 BE PRESENT.

You need to show your active engagement and involvement in every meeting you attend at work.

It is not enough to just attend a meeting and listen to what's being said; you must also be a contributing participant in that meeting. Meetings provide a platform for you to demonstrate your understanding and interest in what's going on in the company. They give you an opportunity to highlight your capabilities through the questions you ask, the contributions you make to the conversation, and how you positively influence the meeting dynamics. Your meeting behavior is an indicator of your work performance and will be interpreted as such.

…And one more thing to remember—you need stay awake, even in large, boring, all employee meetings; falling asleep is unacceptable and inexcusable.

#13 CLEAN OUT THE MICROWAVE.

When the food you microwave at work splatters, clean it up.

Cleaning up after yourself is an implied expectation and a basic common courtesy. For some reason, people do not believe that this behavior applies to microwave splatter at work.

Any behavior you engage in has the potential of influencing people's impression of you. Failure to clean up after yourself has the potential to be projected onto other work characteristics. Unattended microwave splatter turns into:

• Inattentiveness to details

• Inability to produce quality work deliverables

• Lack of pride and ownership

• Failure to be a conscientious team player

You are always being evaluated, always. While someone may not feel comfortable asking you to clean up after yourself, they may feel justified in providing negative feedback on the quality of your work—an opinion piqued because you didn't clean up your microwave splatter.

#14 CHOOSE YOUR TEAMS WISELY.

Some work related teams are more fun to participate on than others. Those teams may include planning the holiday party, the social activities committee, or a team charged with increasing employee morale. Being a member on these teams may break up monotony and bring levity to the workplace; yet it will seldom result in anything other than a 'thank you' and maybe a token gift card.

If you are going to take on more responsibilities in addition to your core work activities, do so selectively. Work on assignments that align with the company or department's strategic initiatives. Ideally, you want to work on initiatives that:

• Directly impact customers

• Affect the bottom line (generates revenue)

• Are developmental opportunities because you are learning a new skill valued by the company

Teams of this nature have greater visibility within the organization and the output from the team's work tends to be valued by leadership. Participants often receive financial rewards for their efforts, including:

• Above average merit increases/pay raises

• Higher bonus payouts/stock options

• Promotional opportunities and other developmental assignments

Remember, while your colleagues may appreciate your efforts and enjoy the fruit of your labor, planning parties will seldom net you performance based rewards.

#15 BECOME AN EXPERT AT SELF-MANAGEMENT.

Self-management: the ability to manage your work independently, without the need for your manager to tell you what to do each step along the way <u>and</u> without the need for your manager to constantly follow-up and track your progress.

Attributes of a self-manager:

• Completes assignments in their entirety; doesn't leave elements of an assignment undone or fail to meet expectations

• Informs manager of action plan to complete assignments

• Keeps manager apprised of assignment status; shares updates prior to manager asking

• Completes assignments on time, always meeting or beating deadlines; if unable to complete the assignment on time, informs manager in advance with an action plan to get the assignment back on track

• Resolves issues related to assignments independently, including technical challenges, interpersonal relationships, and resource limitations

• Engages with manager regularly, providing opportunities for input and coaching

Self-management and initiative are twins; you will rarely, if ever, find one without the other. Make both of them a part of your professional repertoire.

#16 MAKE YOUR MANAGER'S LIFE EASIER.

While you may have been the most qualified person for the role, your manager hired you to help manage his or her workload—namely your work responsibilities. In other words, your manager hired you to make *their* work life easier. Remember that; <u>always</u> remember that.

To make your manager's life easier, you need to be aware of a few things:

• Managers manage up, not down; they work to impress their manager, not you

• Managers dislike dealing with human resources/personnel issues, so don't become one

• Make your manager look good and they will reward

you for your work efforts

Managers are employees, too. They receive performance evaluations, just like you; they want financial rewards for their work efforts, just like you; and they want to be thought of well by their manager, just like you. The degree to which you help your manager achieve their work objectives by doing your job well is the degree to which they will help you achieve your career goals. Become an expert at self-management *(see above)*. Handle your business so your manager won't have to; make them look good and they will reward you for your business efforts.

#17 LEARN HOW TO COMPARTMENTALIZE.

To compartmentalize means to separate into categories or sections. It is a useful skill to have because it helps you manage your emotions and the expression of those emotions appropriately in the workplace.

When you compartmentalize at work, you take the emotions that you are experiencing in your personal life and set them aside while you are at work to focus on your job. In other words, you *leave the emotional drama* from your personal life at home so that the drama does not spill into your work life and negatively affect your job performance.

If someone makes you angry at home, anger and frustration should not show up in how you interact with peers. Sadness because of a family illness or a breakup should not find you weeping uncontrollably at work. Take the time to deal with your personal issues and as needed, inform your manager about the situation. However, when you're at work, focus on work and engaging in the appropriate emotions associated with your job.

#18 ENGAGE HUMAN RESOURCES SELECTIVELY.

Human Resources is not your friend.

Because it is the function within the company responsible for dealing with employee issues, people think HR has the employees' best interests at heart. Not so. HR's primary goal is the effective management of the company's human assets to help the company achieve its strategic objectives (i.e., make money). If in the process of achieving that goal HR helps the employee along the way, great; if not, oh well, as long as no laws are broken.

Just to be clear, HR is not the place you go when you are upset with your manager, teammates make you angry, or you want to vent, whine, or complain about something happening in the company. Trust me, after a few meetings with HR that is exactly what it will sound like—complaining.

Engage human resources when you believe your protected workplace rights have been violated (e.g., discrimination, harassment). Like other functions within the company, HR's responsibility is to promote and protect the company's best interest. The violation of workplace rights puts the company in a precarious position and HR will work to address those concerns.

Remember, just because you do not like your manager, think they're a horrible person, or hate one of your team members, learn to deal with it. Do not go to human resources expecting them to "fix it".

#19 BE PREPARED WHEN OPPORTUNITY KNOCKS.

Skill-up is how I like to refer to it. This means that you are always increasing and sharpening the repertoire of your skills and competencies so that when an opportunity presents itself, you will not be deemed unqualified because you do not have the requisite skill set needed for the opportunity. In other words, you need to prepare for opportunity *before* it arrives, even if you don't know what the opportunity is, where it will come from, when it will come, or how it will come.

• Study to get that certification or professional designation

• Learn a new programming language, software program, or piece of equipment

• Become an expert in a particular area—demonstrate mastery

• Volunteer for a work assignment outside of your regular function to force yourself to learn about another area within the company

Opportunities tend to come suddenly. Skill-up so that when opportunity does come, *and it will come*, you will be prepared to seize it.

#20 DO NOT USE PROFANITY IN THE WORKPLACE.

Just because everyone else may be doing it, including your manager, it is not ok to use profanity in the workplace, and it is definitely not ok to curse at another employee.

Cursing is unprofessional. Given the vast selection of words in the English language to express your emotions, why select a curse word? Ninety-nine out of a hundred people will not be offended by cursing, but for the one person who is, e.g., your new manager or the customer with whom you're trying to close a sales deal, why risk it?

If you choose to curse, do so outside of the workplace and away from colleagues. Remember, you are always being evaluated. <u>Always</u>.

#21 ANYTHING YOU SAY MAY BE HELD AGAINST YOU.

When you send an email message, expect it to go viral; when you leave a voice mail message, expect it to go viral. At all times, *be circumspect* in what you say verbally or in writing, knowing that it may be shared with others.

Never send an angry or emotional email or voice mail message, nor communicate in such a way that your message, on its own, could be interpreted so that it is ruinous to you. When you communicate, think about how your message might read or sound out of context, without you there to explain why you said or responded the way you did. If you need to communicate something of a sensitive nature, that has the potential to lead to political ramifications, or may elicit an emotional response, communicate it in person.

In other words, always communicate with the awareness that what you write or say may be held against you—and potentially go viral.

Morinee Terry

#22 ORGANIZATIONAL POLITICS WILL ALWAYS EXIST. LEARN TO DEAL WITH IT.

Politics in the workplace will always exist. Your goal is to learn how to recognize when the politics are in play, understand them, and then manage the politics to your advantage.

In general, politics is about resources and power. It is the giving and taking of those resources, along with the favor and authority to obtain or allocate those resources. Whether it is world politics or workplace politics, if you want something done, you need the resources to do it (e.g., money, people). Accordingly, those resources have to come from somewhere or somebody; hence, *the politics*.

When you sense resistance or conflict between

38

functional areas or individuals, stop and assess what is at stake for each of the factions involved. If the initiative or action does or does not move forward, who has the potential to lose and who has the potential to gain? What will be lost and what will be gained? How great are the costs of failure or sweet the rewards of success? Think beyond the tangible aspects of what is at stake. Assess individual motives and what matters personally to the various stakeholders. Understand this and you will understand the politics in play.

Your goal is to stay neutral. Provide objective and factual input without choosing sides or aligning yourself with a particular faction. You don't know what you don't know, including who really has the power or how vindictive people may become. Manage the political situation to your advantage by demonstrating a high level of emotional intelligence *(the ability to recognize and manage your own emotions and the emotions of others)* throughout your interactions with others.

Regardless of how the situation is resolved, when it's over, let it be said of you that the quality of your work was excellent, your input insightful, and all parties involved want to work with you again.

#23 BE AMBITIOUS.

Be boldly ambitious.

When you are young in your career, it is the perfect time to experiment. Get as many types of career experiences as possible. Work in different functional areas, in multiple industries, and with various technical tools. Don't be afraid to experiment. Be willing to try something new, even if you have never done it before. Pursue different types of opportunities so that the breadth of your professional experience is wide. By doing this, you will be able to show that you have been exposed to and are knowledgeable about a variety of professional areas.

While expanding the breadth of your professional experiences, you will begin to recognize an area(s) or skill set where you have an interest or natural ability. You will recognize this natural ability because performing a task associated with it is effortless and/or people are always saying you are good at it. When you recognize this natural ability, begin to build depth in this area. Learn as much as you can. Become an expert in that area(s).

Your breadth of experiences, coupled with your depth of expertise, will set you up for long-term career success—and when opportunity knocks, and it will, you'll be prepared to seize it!

ABOUT THE AUTHOR

I am a senior human resources professional with over fifteen years of experience working with Fortune 500 companies. One of the saddest things I have witnessed in organizations is talent being wasted. It is especially heartbreaking to see early career talent being wasted. Bright, energetic and enthusiastic individuals just starting their careers become disillusioned, cynical, and sometimes bitter. To see intelligent, hardworking young professionals dumbed-down, unable to give their best because of the leadership style of their managers, saddens me. Unfortunately, too many managers lack the skills, insight, and awareness to provide timely career advice. *FIRST JOB, NEW CAREER, NOW WHAT? 23 Tips for Guaranteed Career Success* is my attempt to help young professionals rise above the leadership style of managers who are excellent at managing the work but lousy at providing career advice. It is based upon years of observations and working with both managers and young professionals. My desire is that it will provide guidance and inspiration to those just starting their careers, and restore hope to others because they now know what they need to do to progress in their stalled careers.

Sincerely – Morinee Terry